SECRETS OF STORYTELLING

A CREATIVE WRITING WORKBOOK FOR KIDS

100 SHORT FICTION PROMPTS FOR AGES 8-12

Natalie Rompella

Illustrations by Jeanine Murch

ROCKRIDGE PRESS

For general information on our other products and services or to obtain technical support, please contact our Customer Care Department within the United States at (866) 744-2665, or outside the United States at (510) 253-0500.

Rockridge Press publishes its books in a variety of electronic and print formats. Some content that appears in print may not be available in electronic books, and vice versa.

Interior and Cover Designer: Jane Archer
Art Producer: Janice Ackerman
Editor: Alyson Penn
Production Editor: Mia Moran
Illustrations © 2020 by Jeanine Murch
Author Photo © 2020 Jessica Weinstock

ISBN: Print 978-1-64739-134-8 | eBook 978-1-64739-135-5
R0

SECRETS OF STORYTELLING

CONTENTS

HOW TO USE THIS BOOK

"You can make anything by writing."

— C. S. LEWIS

If you're reading this, I'm guessing you like to write. You've figured out the power of words: they can make you laugh until you cry, surprise you so much your jaw drops open, or anger you enough to slam a book closed. When you write, you are harnessing this power. You get to affect how people feel and react to words!

If you're like me, you probably can't get enough of writing. I've written all sorts of books on a variety of subjects, including sled-dog racing, centipedes, and even nanotechnology. I've had a blast making up recipes and brainstorming dog names for an entire sled-dog team.

I've created whole worlds with characters I've shaped and situations I've dreamt up. One little change could have a domino effect on what happens to my characters and the storyline.

With this activity book, I want to help you write more. I've included a whopping 100 writing ideas to fuel your creative powers and help you:

- **uncover new ideas,**
- **warm up your brain before diving into your own piece of writing,**
- **make your writing even stronger by giving you loads of tips and tricks,**
- **discover your writing strengths and style, and**
- **become a master of worlds (whoops—I meant a master of *words* but close enough!).**

Unlike when you read fiction, you are welcome to skip around in this book. Maybe a writing exercise sounds super fun—do it! Or perhaps one chapter doesn't interest you—skip it! Or say you find something you want your friend to try—share it! Use this book however you want.

Writing should be fun. I certainly had fun writing this book. I hope you will enjoy and be inspired by all of the writing ideas just waiting for you in the pages that follow.

YOUR STORY

_____'S

WRITING BOOK

My name is _____.
This book belongs to me. If you find it, you
should/should not *(circle one)* read it.

I enjoy writing as much as I love _____.

I often write stories on paper/on the computer/on a stone tablet/in
toothpaste/_____ *(circle one or add your own)*.

I think a tough subject to write about would be _____.
Here's some more about me:

I prefer to write inside/outside *(circle one)*. I also like to write in my
bedroom/in the rainforest (with an umbrella, of course)/in the desert
(with a water jug nearby) *(circle one or describe where you like to
write)* _____.

I like to write in the morning/around lunchtime/at night when I should
be sleeping *(circle one)*.

I LOVE TO WRITE!

PART 1

The Beginning:
Conquering a Blank Page

Whenever I start something new, I open up my notebook to a blank page. I sit a minute and wonder what to say. How should I begin writing? The first word can be the hardest!

When you are facing a blank page, you just need to begin to write! Start with a word, and then make it a sentence. See if you can add a few more sentences and complete just one measly paragraph. Don't worry about what you're saying just yet. You can even write, "I don't know what to write." Why? Because by simply writing something—*anything*—you're warming up your brain for the really good stuff. The words will begin to flow out of you.

I'm guessing that when you think of your favorite author, you picture them sitting down and masterfully writing sentence after sentence. Maybe you even picture them completing a whole book and not rewriting any of it. FALSE! That's not how it works. All writers revise their sentences and even whole chapters once they've completed their first draft. In fact, sometimes they'll delete a whole chapter altogether (note: this has happened to me!). But when you first begin to write something, you don't need to worry about that. The important thing is to just get started.

YOUR STORY

Sometimes it helps to warm up by doing exercises—writing exercises, that is. One that I really enjoy is meme writing. A meme is a funny picture or phrase that is shared on the Internet. My favorites are images of common things with funny captions underneath that I can relate to. For instance, if you found a picture of a dog wearing a silly-looking turtleneck sweater, you could write something like, "Why I don't like to go to the pet store with Mom" or "Blue is *so* not my color."

On the next page, create your own meme. Find a picture (it can be from a magazine or even one you took yourself) and try writing various humorous captions for it.

PASTE PICTURE HERE

"Being a writer is a very peculiar sort of job: it's always you versus a blank sheet of paper (or a blank screen) and quite often the blank piece of paper wins."

— NEIL GAIMAN

Imagine that you've invited a friend to your home for a sleepover. When they arrive, you open the door but leave them standing there in silence. Not very inviting, right?

Now imagine that, instead, you smile, say hello, and ask your friend to come inside, eat pizza, and watch a movie. You've made your guest feel welcome.

That's what your story's beginning should do. It should make your reader want to enter and stay awhile. We don't want to leave our reader standing in the doorway.

YOUR STORY

"Where's Papa going with that ax?" is the first line of E. B. White's classic story, *Charlotte's Web*. Right away the author has made us feel worried about what's going to happen next. Chances are your favorite books have great beginnings that kept you reading. Find a couple of books that have strong opening lines and write them here.

BOOK TITLE

FIRST LINE

YOUR STORY

What ideas are living in your head right now? Let's see what happens if you just start writing. Set a timer for one minute and write the first thing that you think about. Keep writing until the minute is up.

_____

_____

_____

_____

_____

_____

_____

YOUR STORY

You can begin a story in so many ways:

- **Start with dialogue:** "'Hey, that's my diary!' Emma shrieked. 'Give it back!'"

- **Ask a simple question:** "Does anyone actually like Mondays?"

- **Ask an odd question:** "Who would've thought a pumpkin would determine my destiny?"

- **Describe the main character:** "Dylan was not your ordinary twelve-year-old boy. For one, he was a time traveler."

- **Describe the time of day:** "*Ring!* Finally, gym class was over."

- **Tell the reader something shocking or odd about the main character:** "The day was finally here. The day I'd become a professional clown."

Can you think of other good ways to start a story? Write your examples here.

- _____
- _____
- _____
- _____

YOUR STORY

Choose one of the story starters from the preceding page to begin your own story!

WHAT YOU'LL NEED

One of the great things about writing is you don't need special equipment to do it—no racket, helmet, or shoes with spikes on the bottom. J. K. Rowling didn't even have paper handy when inspiration hit her—she had to write the names of the Hogwarts houses on an airplane barf bag! Don't let the same thing happen to you. Here are some handy items to keep close by for when big ideas strike:

- ○ **Paper: a notebook, some loose-leaf paper, or a composition book (circle which one you prefer). (Personally, I have a pretty clipboard with loose-leaf paper that I *must* write on.)**
- ○ **Writing utensil: find one you *love*: a sparkly pencil, a special pen, or colorful markers (star your favorite).**

That's it! You could survive (as a writer, at least) on a deserted island with these two items. However, it can also be helpful to have:

- ○ **A computer or tablet. Eventually you'll want to type up your masterpiece. It will come in handy when you want to make edits.**
- ○ **This book! There are lots of tips and writing prompts to get your creative juices flowing.**
- ○ **A cozy spot to work, such as _____.**
- ○ **A brain charged with ideas. (We discuss this more on page 19.)**
- ○ **A promise to yourself to write often. Get your ideas out of your head and into this world!**

YOUR STORY

Can you think of any writing equipment or inspiration I forgot to mention in the previous activity? Jot it down here.

- _____
- _____
- _____

YOUR STORY

It can be nice to have an inspiring quote to turn to when you get stuck or are feeling frustrated. If you don't already have one, you can find a bunch on the Internet or ask a parent or friend to recommend something. Write your favorite quote and the author on the lines below.

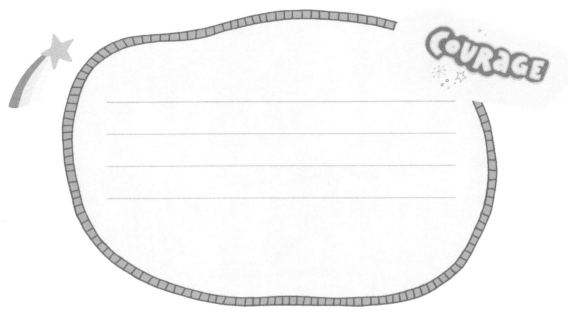

YOUR STORY

Just for fun, write on something you normally wouldn't—the bottom of your shoe (get permission from an adult first), a paper napkin, or an old bookmark. Use what you wrote as the opening lines to a new story.

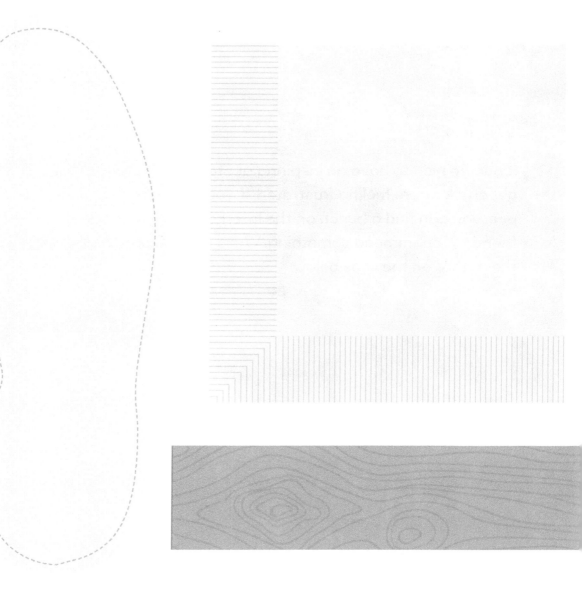

WRITE ANYWHERE

You can write practically anywhere! I often think of story ideas when I'm in the shower, so I keep a pad of waterproof paper and a special pencil there so those ideas don't get lost down the drain. In school, you may be required to write at your desk, but at home you can write just about anywhere you want! I enjoy writing by my fireplace, on my living room floor, and in my backyard on a blanket with my dog. I also bring my notebook with me whenever I go out so I can write at the pool, on a large rock at the park, or at a coffee house—wherever inspiration strikes! Sometimes simply changing the scenery can spark great ideas.

There is no right or wrong way to go about writing. Find a place that works for you. Here are some things you may want to keep in mind when looking for your perfect writing conditions:

- **How's the lighting?** If you've decided to set up camp beneath the dining room table, having a flashlight might help you see better.
- **Are there distractions?** If you've decided to write on the couch in the family room, is your sister or brother watching their favorite show at the same time? You might want to wait until they're napping so you can better concentrate.
- **Does your location inspire you?** Does it help you feel relaxed? My desk is next to a window where I can see my bird feeder. Watching the chickadees or cardinals while I'm thinking about what I'm writing helps put my mind at ease.

YOUR STORY

Look around you. Where can you best focus and write?

Places in your home you like to write:

- _____
- _____
- _____
- _____

Places with too many distractions:

- _____
- _____
- _____
- _____

If you could write anywhere in the world, where would it be and why?

_____
_____
_____
_____

write anywhere

YOUR STORY

Pretend you're writing an ad to get people to come to *The Perfect Place to Write*. Convince your readers to go there. Draw a picture to go with your ad.

THE PERFECT PLACE TO WRITE

"If you want to be a writer, write a little bit every day. Pay attention to the world around you. Stories are hiding, waiting everywhere. You just have to open your eyes and your heart."

— KATE DICAMILLO

I'm going to share a secret with you about writers: we view the world a bit differently. I refer to it as "Writer's Brain." Wherever I go, I find ways to use what I see, hear, smell, touch, and experience in a story. My dog does something silly? Why, that would make a cute picture book! I smell something unusual? I can use the description of that smell in my novel. I just can't turn it off!

Because of my Writer's Brain, I am never short on ideas. The good news is that anyone can develop their Writer's Brain. It just takes practice. Here's a trick to get you going: When you are looking at the world around you, ask yourself, *What if?* Maybe your mom tells you to clean your room—what if you *never* did? What would happen? What would your room look like in a week? Or a year? Picture yourself ten years from now, swimming through all of the clothes and candy wrappers and cereal bowls you forgot to put in the kitchen. Try another one: You're sitting in history class. What if a kid from the 1800s crashed through the ceiling in his time machine and needed your help? Asking *What if?* works to bend just about any situation into an interesting story. After a couple of tries, I bet your brain will be trained to find stories everywhere.

YOUR STORY

You can write a story about so many different things. Here's a list to help you generate some ideas. Add your own ways to start a story at the end of this list.

- A school experience
- A memory from when you were younger
- A wish you have
- A "what if" question
- Something that could happen in the future
- Something that is unlikely to happen in the future
- A view outside the window in your bedroom
- A common problem you and your friends have
- A hobby you have
- A mash-up of two unrelated ideas

- _____
- _____
- _____
- _____
- _____

WRITING IS MAGIC

YOUR STORY

Once you've developed your Writer's Brain, you'll find story ideas all around you. In fact, I bet that you can think of a topic for every letter of the alphabet. For instance, *A* is for *Allowance*—maybe a character tries to find a way to double his allowance. *B* is for *Balloontown*—a town made totally out of balloons. See if you can think of something for each letter. Don't worry if you have to skip some—you can always go back and fill them in later. Feel free to put more than one idea down per letter.

A _____   N _____

B _____   O _____

C _____   P _____

D _____   Q _____

E _____   R _____

F _____   S _____

G _____   T _____

H _____   U _____

I _____   V _____

J _____   W _____

k _____   X _____

L _____   Y _____

M _____   Z _____

YOUR STORY

Have you ever heard of a fractured fairy tale? It's when a fairy tale is twisted, changed, or modernized but keeps some of the same elements—like, say, "Goldilocks and the Three Iguanas." Often the general story stays the same, but the characters or setting are altered. Sometimes the ending changes. What's great about writing a fractured fairy tale is that the storyline has already been laid out for you. You simply get to reimagine parts of it. Do you have a favorite fairy tale? How could you update or change it? Write your idea here.

FAIRY TALE TITLE: _____

"There is only one way
to eat an elephant,
a bite at a time."

— DESMOND TUTU

We've all been there: we sit down to write and *nothing* will come out. It happens to everyone. But there is hope! When this happens to me, I think about *why* it might be occurring. Have I been sitting at my desk too long? Am I hungry? My best solution is often to get up and get moving. I find going for a run or walk outside does the trick. I'm guessing it's both the movement and fresh air that helps.

I'll share another trick I use (and not just with writing but with any difficult task). Currently, I am in the process of finishing a 1,000-piece puzzle on my kitchen table. I have about 30 pieces left—and they're all the tough ones. Each time I walk by, I try to fit in a single piece. Sometimes I end up placing a couple of pieces. I do the same thing with my writing. When I just don't feel like writing, I say to myself, *Just put down one sentence, and then you can go do something different.* Even if it isn't a wonderful sentence, it's something. Often, this will help me get out of my funk, and I'll end up writing a bunch more, maybe even a whole page! I just needed to get over that hump of my brain feeling uninspired.

YOUR STORY

If you are feeling stuck and can't seem to write anything, one of these handy tips might be just the thing to jump-start your writing:

1. Move to a new location to write, maybe even outside.
2. Do something active: go for a walk, play basketball, dance.
3. Read a book.
4. Talk to someone.
5. Interact with a pet.
6. Pretend you're interviewing a character in your story (see page 66 for more on this).
7. Doodle or draw.
8. Eat a healthy snack.
9. Switch to a different writing project.
10. Have someone read what you've written so far.
11. *Just write one more sentence!*

Now add some of your own tips. What are some of the things you like to do to put you back in the writing mood?

12. _____
13. _____
14. _____
15. _____

Motivation

YOUR STORY STASH

"Humans waste words. They toss them like banana peels and leave them to rot. Everyone knows the peels are the best part."

— FROM *THE ONE AND ONLY IVAN* BY KATHERINE APPLEGATE

This is the really fun part of the book! It's where you can keep track of all of your wonderful ideas. Most authors—including myself—have a special notebook or file where they write down words, character descriptions, and story ideas to refer to when they are feeling stuck or want to start something new. Jot down whatever interests you: words, feelings, settings, sounds, names, *What ifs . . .*

YOUR STORY

_____'S VERY IMPORTANT CONTRACT THAT WILL NEVER EVER BE BROKEN

I _____ **(write name)** promise to use this section of the book to capture my writing ideas. It doesn't matter if it's bright and early in the morning or so dark at night that I need a flashlight to see; I will write my ideas down!

I also promise to allow all ideas into my head and into this book without judging them as good or bad. I reserve the right to change some of them and dismiss others at a later time, but I will always write my ideas down as they come to me.

I will think of myself as an awesome/amazing/ fantastic/_____ **(circle all that apply and/or insert your own description here)** writer.

_____

(signature here)

HAVING FUN WITH WORDS

Words are the building blocks of great writing. Specific words and how they are combined can make or break a sentence. Read the first sentence of your favorite book. Imagine if the author took some of those words out—it wouldn't feel the same. Here's the first sentence from one of my favorite books, *The Meanest Doll in the World* by Ann M. Martin and Laura Godwin:

> "Annabelle Doll sat in the soap dish high above the bathtub in the Palmers' house."

What if the authors had written, "A doll was in a bathroom at a house"? It's just not the same image! I love all of the attention to detail here: the doll's fun name; that she's not only in a soap dish but *sitting* in a soap dish; and that I know whose house she's in. The doll already has personality.

Let's have some fun collecting words. Keep track of words you enjoy saying (such as *cacophony*), words that provoke wonderful images (*sea glass* for me!), silly-sounding words (*persnickety* works here), or combinations that will make for an interesting story (*pink dolphins*).

YOUR STORY

Write your favorite words in the space that follows. Feel free to borrow from your favorite novels, songs, or even picture books.

YOUR STORY

A fun way to collect words is by reading magazines or newspapers. Choose a page and cut out fun words you find. Arrange them to make a sentence. Paste your sentence here.

YOUR STORY

Using the sentence you made in the preceding exercise, write the beginning of a new short story.

YOUR STORY

Sight, hearing, smell, taste, and touch—there are so many ways to describe something using your senses. Let's brainstorm fun words that describe things using our senses. For example, color. How about *lilac* or *puce*? What about sound words? Say, *grinding* or *staccato*? Write your favorite words below and refer to this list when you want to add more detail to a story.

Sight descriptions (color, pattern, shape)

_____ _____ _____

_____ _____ _____

_____ _____ _____

_____ _____ _____

_____ _____ _____

Sound descriptions (volume, pitch)

_____ _____ _____

_____ _____ _____

_____ _____ _____

_____ _____ _____

Taste descriptions (flavor, texture)

_____ _____ _____
_____ _____ _____
_____ _____ _____
_____ _____ _____

Smell descriptions (specific fragrance, strength of a smell)

_____ _____ _____
_____ _____ _____
_____ _____ _____
_____ _____ _____

Touch descriptions (temperature, firmness, texture)

_____ _____ _____
_____ _____ _____
_____ _____ _____
_____ _____ _____

MAKING A MOOD BOARD

A mood board is a kind of collage that people make to capture images and words that inspire them. Your bedroom walls may act as your mood board with artwork or pictures, photos of friends, etc. on them. On my desk I keep pictures of my children and dog, a figurine I bought in Alaska, and an inspiring quote. Mood boards can provide comfort, motivate you, and spark creativity.

YOUR STORY

Collect personal photos, pictures you like from magazines, or meaningful or funny headlines, or draw images of things that inspire you. Paste them into the space provided on the next page to create your very own **Writer's Mood Board**.

MY MOOD BOARD

YOUR STORY

If you aren't able to cut out images, or maybe you just aren't in the mood to draw that fabulous sunset you picture in your head, describe your favorite characters, settings, or scenarios that inspire you to write.

-
-
-
-
-
-
-
-
-
-
-
-

CARING FOR YOUR IDEAS

I'm guessing that while you've been reading about all the ways to start a story, you've already come up with some story ideas of your own. Your ideas may just be in bits and pieces right now—that's fine. I started writing down all of my random ideas in 2015. I now have over 180! Sometimes when I feel like starting a new project, I revisit my list. I have turned some of these ideas into completed stories. Other times, my list helps me think of new ideas. For instance, if I wrote down, "a boy learning to ride a bicycle," I may instead think about writing a story where a boy loses his bike at the park and doesn't want to tell his parents, a girl's bike getting a flat tire on her way to the big game, or even a horse who wishes he could ride a bike (hey, that's not a bad idea!).

Although you may say to yourself, *I'll remember that idea*, you might not. Remember your Very Important Contract on page 30.

YOUR STORY

Take some time to look at your mood board, then write all of the random but brilliant ideas that fill your brain here.

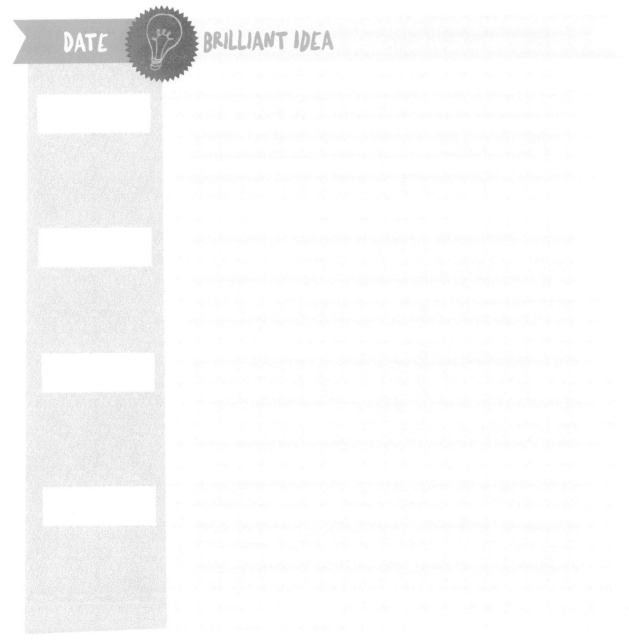

DATE

BRILLIANT IDEA

YOUR STORY

Similar to fractured fairy tales (page 22), book and movie titles can be great fodder for the imagination. Changing just one word can set you on the path to a hilarious new story! For instance, instead of *Charlotte's Web*, what about *Charlotte's Donut? The Lion, the Witch, and the Wardrobe* could be changed to *The Lion, the Witch, and the Refrigerator*. Just imagine what takes place inside that fridge! *Anne of Green Olives, The Ninja of Oz, Ranger in Love* . . . I could go on forever! See what you can come up with. Change four titles.

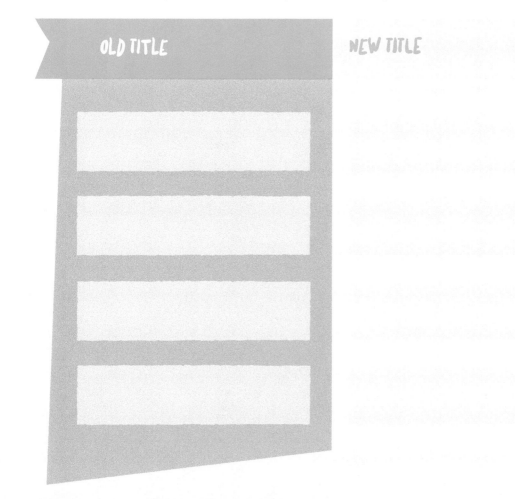

OLD TITLE

NEW TITLE

YOUR STORY

All books feature text on the back cover or flap that's intended to quickly summarize the story, capture our interest, and convince us to read the book. Choose one of your titles from the preceding exercise and then try writing your own book description for it.

The Middle:
Building Worlds

In this section of the book we're focusing on what happens after you settle on an idea: world building! Can you feel the power coursing through your veins? When you write fiction, you are in charge of creating a whole world! That "world" can be a simple one with people just like yourself in a school similar to yours, or it can be a world with dragons and fairies and quicksand. It's up to you! You get to decide on everything: the setting, the characters, what problems they'll face, and how they overcome those problems.

What's nice about world building is you can easily change your mind as your story unfolds. Nothing is set in stone.

YOUR STORY

What are some worlds you enjoy or would enjoy visiting from books, movies, or your imagination? Write them in the boxes below.

CHARACTERS

"'Real isn't how you are made,' said the Skin Horse. 'It's a thing that happens to you. When a child loves you for a long, long time, not just to play with, but REALLY loves you, then you become Real.'"

— FROM *THE VELVETEEN RABBIT* BY MARGERY WILLIAMS

Have you ever been thinking of someone but just couldn't put your finger on where you knew them from, only to realize the person was actually a character from a book you've read? This has happened to me on numerous occasions. The author made the character seem so real, so authentic, that I felt I personally knew them. To create characters that leap off the page, you need to think about all of the details that make them unique.

Growing up, I had a doll named Elbertina. Elbertina was quite a boisterous doll. I would have her walk, play, and talk as if she were real. She had likes (anything banana flavored) and dislikes (being quiet, for one). My older sister would often be entertained with what Elbertina did and said. Once she even complained to my parents that her dolls weren't alive like mine were. We all treated Elbertina as one of the family. This is what we want when we create a character—it should feel like they're actually alive.

To become a stronger writer, figure out what makes the characters from your favorite books come to life. When I wrote *Cookie Cutters & Sled Runners*, I wanted my main character's guinea pig to "come to life." Here's what I wrote: "The minute I saw Bernie Toast, I fell in love . . . a nameless guinea pig with wiry, pitch-black fur . . . And he'd been staring at me, waiting for a home."

YOUR STORY

Who are your favorite characters from books or movies? Make a list here.

- _____
- _____
- _____
- _____
- _____
- _____
- _____
- _____

YOUR STORY

The names that you give your characters are important details. Names can help tell us where the character is from and even help set the tone of the story. Is your character serious? If so, you might want a name that reflects that. Are they funny? Sometimes giving a character a very serious name makes them even funnier. My favorite characters to name are dogs. They can have human names (how about Natalie?), be named after places (picture a dachshund named Chattanooga), or even have food names (Meatball works with most pooches). Come up with some character names below.

THE VILLAIN

_____

_____

_____

THE PRINCESS

_____

_____

_____

THE COURT JESTER

_____

_____

_____

A FANCY CAT

_____

_____

_____

A TROUBLEMAKING SLOTH

_____

_____

_____

AN INTELLIGENT WORM

_____

_____

_____

YOUR STORY

Choose two of the characters you named in the preceding exercise and imagine them on their phones texting each other back and forth about going glamping together (that's fancy camping)! For example, what would a worm and a court jester text to each other as they prepare for the trip? Maybe what food to bring? What clothes to pack? Be sure to use their new names and remember: text messages are short and to the point!

YOUR STORY

You can make your characters more interesting simply by mashing up funny and unusual details about how they like to spend their time—say, a disco-dancing fish who likes to bake snickerdoodle cookies. In the space below, come up with six different characters of your own.

ADJECTIVE	CHARACTER	WHO LIKES TO . . .
A describing word, such as happy, fuzzy, or invisible	Type of person, animal, or thing	Name of an activity
1.	1.	1.
2.	2.	2.
3.	3.	3.
4.	4.	4.
5.	5.	5.
6.	6.	6.

YOUR STORY

Let's do more character mash-ups using the details you imagined in the last exercise! Get three dice and assign one to each column (Adjective, Character, Who likes to . . .). Roll the dice and then write down one word per column to see what kind of crazy character random selection makes. Do this as many times as you like. Then write a description of that character.

OBSERVING THE WORLD AROUND YOU

Writers often base their characters on themselves or people they know. This requires the power of observation, which is just a fancy way of saying noticing the unique characteristics about people and things around you.

What sorts of things do you notice about the people in your life? Of course you can observe things about what they look like and wear, but also start to notice their interests, how they move, what they say, and how they say it. What makes your little brother laugh? How does your mom style her hair? What shoes does the postal carrier wear?

For instance, I cannot stand watching people brush their teeth in movies and on TV. It grosses me out! However, I can look at creepy crawlies all day long. (I actually collect insects!) If I were a character in a story, I might cringe as someone brushes their teeth but then have a pet hissing cockroach (which I did!).

Things to observe about the people in your life:

- **Their hair: the style, color, length**
- **What they like to snack on**
- **What makes them laugh**
- **How they stand: tall, hunched over, hand on hip**
- **How they dress: casual, sporty, dressy, trendy**
- **Their nervous habit: biting their nails, tapping their foot**

YOUR STORY

Review the preceding list. What other types of things do you think you can observe about people? Write them below.

- _____
- _____
- _____
- _____
- _____
- _____
- _____
- _____
- _____

YOUR STORY

Choose someone in your family and then write a description of them without ever mentioning their name. When you are done, read it to your family and have them guess who you wrote about. Be sure to keep it positive!

_____

_____

_____

_____

_____

_____

_____

YOUR STORY: Picture This

Have you ever found a photo of someone you didn't know and wondered what they were like? A great way to dig deeper into a character is to use a picture prompt. For each of the pictures that follow, give yourself two minutes to write down as much as you can about the character—a.k.a. their backstory. It may include their name, age, where they live, and what they like to do.

_____

_____

_____

_____

_____

_____

_____

_____

_____

_____

_____

_____

_____

_____

_____

_____

_____

_____

_____

_____

YOUR STORY

What if *you* were a character in one of your favorite stories? Pick a scene from a book you like and insert yourself into it. Imagine what it would be like to have the character see you for the first time. How would they describe you?

_____ *(name of a character from a book)*

walked into the room and saw _____ *(your name)* standing there . . .

_____

_____

_____

_____

_____

_____

_____

_____

_____

_____

_____

_____

_____

_____

_____

GETTING TO KNOW YOUR CHARACTERS

The best book characters seem to jump off the page because they have so much personality. But sometimes when we are writing, characters come out flat or a little dull. One way to remedy this is to think of your characters as real people. Spend a day reflecting on what your character would do in daily situations:

- **It's breakfast time.** What would your main character eat? Maybe they're so busy they just grab a banana and go.
- **The teacher returns a math test.** What grade would your main character have gotten? How would they have reacted to their score?

Although the answers to these questions probably won't make it into your story, knowing them will help you better understand your character and visualize how they behave in the world you have created for them.

YOUR STORY

Interviews are a great way to get to know someone. TV reporters do it all the time! Choose one of the characters pictured on pages 60 to 63. Pretend you are interviewing that character by filling out a Character Survey for them.

1. What's your name?

_____

2. How old are you?

_____

3. Where do you live?

_____

4. Do you have many casual friends or a couple of close friends?

_____

5. What do you enjoy doing?

_____

6. What are you scared of?

_____

7. What's your favorite season?

_____

8. What's your favorite food?

_____

9. What's your favorite board game?

_____

10. What questions do you have for me?

_____

YOUR STORY

Now interview a completely new character. You can make one up on the spot or choose one you made in the table on page 55. There are even lines to add your own questions.

1. What's your name?

2. How old are you?

3. Where do you live?

4. Who do you live with?

5. What are some sports or hobbies you enjoy?

6. Do you like dogs or cats better? Why?

7. Do you like to ride roller coasters? Why or why not?

_____

8. _____ ?

_____

9. _____ ?

_____

10. _____ ?

_____

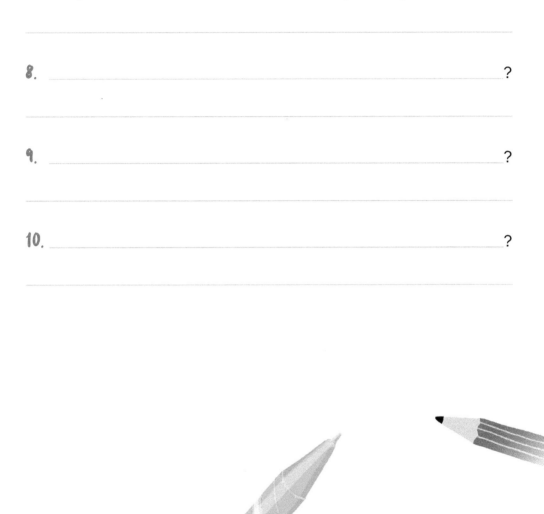

YOUR STORY

Choose one of the two characters from the preceding exercise to start a story where the character finds a hundred-dollar bill on the sidewalk. Knowing the character's personality, how will they react? What will they do? Write it in the space that follows.

YOUR STORY

Let's write a poem about a character you'd like to create.
Choose a name, then write the letters of that name down
the left side of the paper. For each letter of the name, write
a descriptive detail about your character. (This is called an
acrostic poem.) Here's an example about a lizard named Sam:

Selfish
Adventurous
Makes music on the guitar

FIGURING OUT MOTIVATION

In order to keep a story moving, our characters need to be doing something. More importantly, they need to have a reason they're doing what they're doing. This is called *motivation*. For example: Why did four siblings climb inside a wardrobe? Why does a pigeon want to drive a bus? Why does the prince search for the owner of the glass slipper? The answer to each of these questions tells us what motivated each character to do what they did. Some common motivations include love, anger, acceptance, curiosity, and guilt, but there are many, many more.

Why might you go into the kitchen and grab an apple? Probably because you are hungry. Why does your mom give you a hug? Because she loves you. Why is the baby crying? That's a tough one. Parents spend a lot of time trying to figure out the motivation of babies since they can't tell us. Are they hungry, wet, tired? It's not always easy to know. You don't want your characters to be so hard to figure out.

YOUR STORY

I've listed some story ideas below, but they each need a motive. Read the scenario and then write down why the character might have done the action. There's no right or wrong answer here! Get creative.

1. A boy rides a roller coaster because

2. A girl writes an apology letter to her next-door neighbor because

3. A bear growls at a hummingbird because

4. A child programs a robot to do chores for him because

YOUR STORY

Are you familiar with the story "Goldilocks and the Three Bears"? The author of that story never tells us why Goldilocks decided to take a walk in the woods in the first place. Write a backstory for Goldilocks in the space below. Tell us why she took a walk and how she ended up in the bears' house.

WRITE ANYWHERE

"I, Willy Wonka, have decided to allow five children—just five, mind you, and no more—to visit my factory this year. These lucky five will be shown around personally by me, and they will be allowed to see all the secrets and the magic of my factory."

— FROM *CHARLIE AND THE CHOCOLATE FACTORY* BY ROALD DAHL

*T*he plot thickens! Have you ever heard that before? Or maybe lived it? Something crazy happens and then something even *crazier* happens. The *plot* of a story is simply what happens. Good stories have strong plots with lots of twists and turns. So-so stories do not. Imagine that there's a big sheepdog who wears glasses and fancy shoes and carries a lunch box in her mouth. Can you picture her in your head? What's she doing? Just sitting there? Maybe now have her walking. And walking. Should we keep having her just walk? No. Something needs to happen so we have a story with a plot. Maybe her glasses fall off and break. (We're getting warmer!) This dog (let's name her Sprinkles) was on her way to school to audition for *The Wizard of Oz*, but without her glasses she won't be able to read the script. What if she doesn't get the part of Dorothy? What if they give her the part with no lines—the part of Toto? We have the beginning of a plot!

Plots are the lifeline to any story. Something happens that makes the reader want to continue reading to see how it's resolved. It can be thought of as the beginning, middle, and end, or the main events of a story. In our case, we have Sprinkles who is on her way to school—that's our beginning. But then—*gasp!*—on the way there she trips and her glasses fly off her face, land on the sidewalk, and break. Maybe Sprinkles tries to fix the glasses, or she tries to "borrow" her friend's glasses, or she auditions for the school play without them! There's the story we're going to tell. In the end, there needs to be some sort of resolution. We don't want our reader to feel disappointed.

YOUR STORY

Think about books and movies you've enjoyed. One aspect that probably made them so terrific is that they had a great storyline—something pretty exciting happened and kept you interested throughout. To top it off, they each had a satisfying ending. List the plotlines from some of your favorite books or movies in the space below. I included my own favorite as an example.

BOOK/MOVIE	PLOTLINE
E.T. the Extra-Terrestrial	Alien gets left behind on Earth. With the help of an Earthling, he tries to get back to his home planet.

YOUR STORY

Oh no! The book and movie plotlines you listed in the previous exercise just got all mixed up! Choose two plotlines to combine. Then write a description about the new story.

BRAINSTORMING STORYLINES

Like ideas, plots can sprout from anywhere. They can be simple, such as a story about a boy who thinks the house next to his is haunted, or complex, such as a story about a knight on a quest who faces dragons and saves the kingdom.

Sometimes plots come together from a *What if?* (Remember those from page 19?) What if I worked at an ice-cream parlor and the power went off and all the ice cream was going to melt and I had to come up with a solution so it didn't turn into an ice-cream pool? Other times, plots are considered character-driven. The character struggles—things get worse before they get better—but, in the end, through the struggles, the character changes.

YOUR STORY: Picture This

Look at the pictures that follow. For each, write a short plot (similar to a movie trailer or a book jacket description).

_____

_____

_____

_____

_____

_____

_____

_____

YOUR STORY

Think about something strange that occurred recently—maybe an unexplained sound or something you saw on the sidewalk that was unidentifiable. Turn that experience into a short story.

YOUR STORY

Think of everyday situations in your life that
you could make into a *What if?* For instance,
my dog just came into my office and poked her
snout into a bag on the floor. What if she goes
through *all* my stuff when I'm not home? Maybe she
uses my computer and wears my lipstick! What could you turn
into a *What if?* Brainstorm in the space below.

THE PLOT
THICKENS

- What if _____

  _____ ?

- What if _____

  _____ ?

- What if _____

  _____ ?

- What if _____

  _____ ?

- What if _____

  _____ ?

YOUR STORY

Choose a *What if?* from the list you made in the preceding exercise and turn it into a short story.

BORROWING FROM YOUR OWN LIFE

A lot of writers like to borrow situations from their real life and turn them into stories. Along the way, they make up details to keep it interesting for the reader. Here are some tips for how to turn a real-life situation into a fictional story:

- **Change the character of the situation. Don't make the character a replica of you. Maybe give him or her some qualities you wished you had or make the character the exact opposite of you.**

- **Change the outcome. Sometimes a situation makes a great story, but the ending wasn't that memorable. Make it more exciting.**

- **Take out unnecessary details. Maybe in real life you and your friends were making grilled cheese sandwiches and all the bread burned, but it doesn't really have anything to do with the story. Does it move the plot along? If not, remove it.**

- **Swap out a so-so setting for a more exciting one. Instead of something happening in your kitchen, place the characters at a roller rink, the beach, or a skate park.**

- **Remove people who were really there but make the scene more complicated. This is always a tough one. Let's say you are fictionalizing a situation that happened with you and six of your friends, but really, it only affected three of you. By writing in all seven people, you have to keep mentioning each, having each person say something, etc. Instead, maybe morph two of your friends into one: make the character talk like Katie but look like Avery.**

YOUR STORY

Think of a situation you've been in that would make a good story. What could you change about it?

WHAT HAPPENED?

DETAILS I MIGHT CHANGE

YOUR STORY

Time to turn fact into fiction! Pick one of the real-life "What happened?" scenarios you wrote in the preceding exercise and fictionalize it! Have fun. Change your friends' names and the location it took place (where have you always wished you lived?); maybe even change your pet fish to a horse!

YOUR STORY

Sometimes real life gets in the way of writing. Something so big is happening that you don't have a lot of time to write. However, you may still want to get your thoughts down on paper. If you have something big happening in your life right now and want to get it out of your head, write it here. Of course, you can also fictionalize it.

USING TENSION AND CONFLICT TO YOUR ADVANTAGE

For those of you who enjoy roller coasters, imagine riding one that has a very high hill at the beginning. The car goes up and up and up. But what if that was it—the ride just ended there? You had built up all this excitement, but you never got to go racing down. Or, what if you boarded a roller coaster and all it did was go straight? If you were anticipating lots of loop-de-loops and intense hills, you might be disappointed.

Writing a good story is a lot like a good amusement park ride. You want your reader to feel anticipation for what happens next. This is called *tension*. And then you need something significant to happen, for something to go wrong or for there to be a problem that needs to be solved (or a relationship that needs saving). This is called *conflict*. For example, if my story is about a girl and her new baby brother, something must go wrong. Maybe she always has to babysit and misses the big school dance, or she's up all night listening to her brother cry and is always tired—so tired she falls asleep and misses her big figure-skating competition.

Tension and conflict keep our plot interesting and our readers, well, reading.

YOUR STORY

Some sample conflicts are listed below. Think of other conflicts from your real life or simply make them up (what sorts of problems might a dragon tamer have, anyway?)! Add them to the end of the list.

- **Problems with friends**
- **Problems with family members**
- **Situations in school**
- **Natural disasters**
- **Problems with how the character sees themselves**

- _____

- _____

- _____

- _____

YOUR STORY

Choose a character from pages 81 to 84. Think of a conflict that might happen to that character. For instance, what problems might that alien have now that he's on a foreign planet? Or make up something totally outrageous—maybe the alien becomes the star of the basketball team but doesn't know how to keep score!

_____

(Name of Character)

_____

_____

_____

_____

_____

_____

_____

_____

RAISING THE STAKES

Do you ever watch game shows on TV? Sometimes the contestant needs to answer lots of tough questions. With each question, the amount of money awarded increases. Often I'm about to turn off the TV, but then I need to know—will the woman win the million dollars? The contestant may win $100 on question one, $1,000 on the next question, and so on. If the show had just started with the million-dollar prize, I would have watched the first few minutes and then turned it off. The producers prevent that from happening by raising the stakes. They start small and increase the drama or excitement throughout the show.

You should do this when you write stories. Don't begin with your big splash. Instead, start small and work your way up through more difficult challenges, increasingly more humorous situations, etc., saving the best and biggest for last—that's your million-dollar prize.

YOUR STORY

Five characters are listed below. What are the most outrageous or difficult situations you can imagine for each of them?

A king _____

An explorer _____

A pet rabbit _____

A baker _____

You _____

YOUR STORY

I bet you have some great ideas for that king or pet rabbit in the previous exercise. Choose one and turn it into a story.

_____

_____

_____

_____

_____

_____

Q&A time. Here are some common questions writers ask about plot, and the answers.

Do you have to write in chronological order?

For something you're writing in school, you might need to. But when you're writing for yourself, absolutely not! Maybe you're angry and want to write the angry scene for your story before you've even introduced the characters. Go for it! Use that energy for good. Beginnings are often the most difficult to write. Move on to the juicy stuff and go back to the beginning later.

Do you have to know exactly where your story will go before you start writing?

There are generally two types of writers: plotters and pantsers. Plotters map out the entire story either before beginning or early on. Pantsers, for the most part, "fly by the seat of their pants." A true pantser starts writing without knowing exactly where the story is headed. They let their characters show them the way. Of course, many writers also fall somewhere in between. Do what works for you.

How much should you have happening in your story?

You've learned about plots, but there can also be subplots, or side stories. Think back to when your parents read you picture books. Those stories featured one main problem or issue. Now think of some of the more complex novels you've read. In addition to the main storyline, other things are happening—maybe a situation with a friendship or the family. Those are subplots.

Like picture books, short stories often do not have subplots simply because there isn't enough space to resolve more than one conflict (see page 93). When writing short stories, I recommend that you stick to just having one main plot. I find that it is more satisfying to complete a story than to write one that gets out of hand and never ends. But feel free to prove me wrong.

CLIFFHANGER 101

Years ago, my friend brought me into his kitchen. "What is *this*?" he asked, opening up his cupboard. I looked inside and gasped.

Do you want to know what I saw? That is the power of a cliffhanger.

Should you always use cliffhangers in your stories? If you use them too much, they're not as exciting, kind of like that story about the boy who cried wolf: in the end, no one believed him. If you use cliffhangers sparingly, they really stand out.

As for *ending* your story on a cliffhanger, you want to be careful. Slapping a "to be continued" on the last page can sometimes seem like you didn't know how to end your story. Take a look at books you enjoy that are part of a series to see how the author wraps them up. How did they end things? Did they maybe hint at some loose ends?

Speaking of loose ends . . . when I looked in the cupboard, I was surprised to find what resembled a two-foot-tall Jack-and-the-Beanstalk-looking vine. It wound around the inside of the shelf. Turns out, it was a very old forgotten potato that had sprouted out of control!

YOUR STORY

Try your hand at turning these sentences into cliffhangers. Then write some of your own. The first one is done for you.

1. Demi smiled and said, "Shhh . . . We can't let anyone know." She opened the door and my jaw dropped open.

2. Tristin raced over to the edge of the woods where he

3. Cupcake scampered over and

4. The flying car

5.

6.

7.

YOUR STORY

Pick one of the preceding cliffhangers and turn it into a short story.

"The cyclone had set the house down, very gently—for a cyclone—in the midst of a country of marvelous beauty. There were lovely patches of greensward all about, with stately trees bearing rich and luscious fruits."

— FROM *THE WONDERFUL WIZARD OF OZ* BY L. FRANK BAUM

ave you ever read a book where you felt a little lost? Maybe the author never told you where you were. I've been accused by my writer friends of forgetting to add enough details about the setting in a scene. The poor characters were left floating in an unknown place.

Setting includes both place and time. The place can be a very large geographical location, such as on Jupiter, or it can be minuscule, such as inside a flower. A setting also tells us *when* a story takes place. It could be set in 1952 or 2591. Even a detail such as it being Wednesday might be important to the story. Maybe the talent show takes place on Friday and we now know the main character has only two days to make up with her friend with whom she's doing a duet.

YOUR STORY

What are some of your favorite settings from books and movies? Share a couple of them below, describing the setting.

BOOK/MOVIE	SETTING

YOUR STORY

How many different settings can you think of within your town (playground, ravine, pool . . .)? Name as many as you can in two minutes.

FUN

YOUR STORY

Historical fiction is set in the past. Often it focuses on a significant event, such as World War I or the sinking of the *Titanic*. Make a list of historical events that interest you. Feel free to add to this list later if you learn about a really cool story in history class!

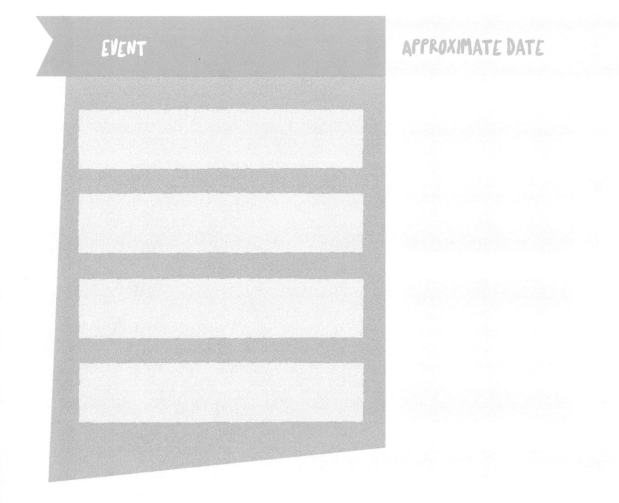

EVENT	APPROXIMATE DATE

LOCATION, LOCATION, LOCATION

When I was in sixth grade, a nearby town's schools flooded. With the severity of damage, the students had to be relocated. Shockingly, the new temporary school was a shopping mall! One of the big department stores had permanently closed, so desks were brought in and different sections were turned into classrooms.

There are a lot of books about school—school dances, failing a big test, a disagreement with a friend. They almost always take place in a regular classroom. Instead, picture each of those situations in a mall classroom. Being in a mall adds another layer to the plot. (By the way, author Jamie Gilson wrote a novel called *Hobie Hanson, Greatest Hero of the Mall* that is based on just this situation.)

Isn't it amazing how setting can alter a story? Think of how location can change the way a story feels. Imagine how different a scene would be if it took place in the character's bedroom versus at an amusement park or on a space station.

YOUR STORY

Change the location in some of your favorite stories. For instance, in *Charlie and the Chocolate Factory*, what if Charlie didn't get a Golden Ticket to a chocolate factory but to somewhere scary, such as an abandoned carnival? Ready, set, change!

BOOK/MOVIE	ORIGINAL SETTING	NEW SETTING

YOUR STORY: Picture This

Choose one of the characters shown in the following section. Imagine that they just found a time machine. Write three to five sentences about where they decide to travel and why.

_____

_____

_____

_____

_____

_____

_____

_____

YOUR STORY

There are so many ways to change up a story's setting. Think about the following opposites:

- day vs. night
- inside vs. outside
- in public vs. in private
- a stationary location vs. a moving location (a car or airplane)
- a fancy restaurant vs. a greasy spoon diner
- under the sea vs. on land vs. in the air

Select one set of opposite settings from the list above. Now choose one of the following situations:

- hiding from someone or something
- discovering a never-before-seen creature
- uncovering a hidden passageway

Write a scene featuring the first setting in the pair you selected and the situation you chose (for example, it's **daytime** and a character is hiding from someone).

_____

_____

_____

_____

_____

_____

Now write the same scene but change the setting to its opposite (the situation and all other details must stay the same; for example, now it's **nighttime** and your character is hiding from someone).

OPPOSITE SCENE

_____

_____

_____

_____

_____

Do you notice how the change in setting alters the feel of the story? Which setting do you like better?

YOUR STORY

Bloop! You have just entered the body of your favorite book character. As this character, imagine standing outside the front door to your home. Answer the following questions as seen through the eyes of that character.

1. What's your name?

_____

2. What do you think of the entryway?

_____

3. Go into the kitchen. Look around. What do you think?

_____

4. Go into the bedroom of the person whose body you've entered. What do you like about it?

_____

5. What would you change?

_____

6. Would this home suit you? Why or why not?

_____

7. If you could live anywhere in (or out of) this world, where would it be?

_____

8. _____?

_____

9. _____?

_____

10. _____?

_____

YOUR STORY

Have you left your bedroom within the last 24 hours? I'm guessing you've at least visited four locations (the bathroom and kitchen count!). Write down five places you've been in the last day or so.

1. _____

2. _____

3. _____

4. _____

5. _____

YOUR STORY

Choose one of the locations from the previous exercise and jazz it up! Make it bigger, more outrageous, more kid-friendly than it really is. For instance, instead of your normal bathroom, you could write, "My bathroom is the size of a basketball court. It has a tub with a diving board and a water slide. There are palm trees surrounding the sink, which is a waterfall." Or do the opposite—make it worse than it is. "My backyard is teeny tiny. I can hardly put two feet down, and there are two birds circling my head as I speak." Write five sentences exaggerating just where you've been.

I chose to write about _____.

_____

_____

_____

_____

_____

_____

_____

_____

YOUR STORY

Fantasy books can transport you to other worlds where setting often plays a big role. Think of fantasy books you've read and where they take place. Describe a setting from some of your favorite fantasy books and movies.

BOOK/MOVIE	SETTING DESCRIPTION

YOUR STORY

To write a fantasy story, you need to think about the world you're creating. Who are the characters? What are the rules for the world? What does the world look like? Fill out the following survey to brainstorm an idea for a fantasy story.

1. Will your story take place in the past, present, or future?

_____

2. What kinds of characters live there?

_____

3. What villains will there be?

_____

4. Will the story take place on Earth or somewhere else?

_____

5. What magical elements will there be?

_____

6. What rules are there for this world?

_____

7. Roughly how many different major locations exist there?

_____

8. Choose the main setting in your book and describe it.

_____

_____

_____

_____

_____

_____

_____

YOUR STORY

Sometimes it's useful to draw a map of the world you've created. Using the information you came up with in the last activity, draw a map of your fantastical world.

YOUR STORY

Now that you have brainstormed a fantasy story, start writing it! Even if fantasy isn't your thing, see if you can write
10 sentences. You can start at the beginning, at the climax,
or even at the end! Who knows? Maybe you'll be the next
J. R. R. Tolkien!

USING ALL FIVE SENSES

I love watching baking shows—especially when they make cupcakes. Not only do I enjoy seeing the contestants' clever takes on a theme, but I like hearing what kinds of cupcakes they make, such as a vanilla bean cake with lemon curd filling and lemon buttercream. *Yum!* Although I didn't get to personally eat it (hopefully someday that technology will exist!), I felt like I did. The detailed description of the cupcakes is enough to make my mouth water.

When we provide sensory details, our readers can feel as though they're experiencing taste, touch, smell, sight, and sound—it's as if they're actually in the story.

YOUR STORY

Time to go on a scavenger hunt. You are looking for passages in books or magazines that make you feel as if you're experiencing something through one of your senses. Try to find an example for each sense.

SENSE	BOOK/MAGAZINE	WORDS USED
TASTE		
TOUCH		
SMELL		
SIGHT		
SOUND		

YOUR STORY

Imagine going to the following locations. Add sensory detail for each.

A FOOTBALL FIELD ON A RAINY DAY

What you see: _____

What you hear: _____

What you taste: _____

What you touch: _____

What you smell: _____

A HOT AIR BALLOON RIDE IN THE SERENGETI

What you see: _____

What you hear: _____

What you taste: _____

What you touch: _____

What you smell: _____

A CEMETERY ON AN AUTUMN NIGHT

What you see: _____

What you hear: _____

What you taste: _____

What you touch: _____

What you smell: _____

MAKE UP ONE OF YOUR OWN

Location: _____

What you see: _____

What you hear: _____

What you taste: _____

What you touch: _____

What you smell: _____

YOUR STORY

Now choose one of the places from the preceding exercise and write a description of the scene as if you were there this very moment. Try to use all five senses!

USE ALL
5
SENSES

IT'S ALL IN THE DETAILS

Providing robust details about the setting is great, but can there be too much of a good thing? Have you ever read a book where the description went on too long, so you skipped over it? I have. The trick is to give enough details so readers can picture where they are, but then leave some room for them to fill in the holes with their imagination. However, when you're writing your first draft, include anything you want. You can always go back and trim later.

Sensory detail can help us feel like we're there, but try to use details that make sense: If the scene takes place in the kitchen, you could mention the smell of something in the oven. But if the scene takes place in the living room, the smells might not be as necessary. Same with touch: At the ocean, it's great to mention all the things the character feels—the cold water, the gritty sand, the sun beating down. In the living room: not so much.

You may be surprised to hear this, but sometimes adjectives and adverbs just aren't needed and can even sound clunky: "The four-foot-eight-inch-tall girl with the brown, curly hair and purple glasses and jeans with a hole in the knee walked slowly into the room that had four tables and eight chairs." Sometimes less is more.

YOUR STORY

In the paragraphs that follow, cross out what you feel is unneeded detail about the setting and/or characters.

1. Mia opened the enormous metal door to the silver space-ship using the handle that turned clockwise. Her brown eyes were surprisingly shocked. The ground was covered in a layer of dense fog. She stepped down wearing her white space boots that she purchased on sale three weeks ago. The ground squished beneath her feet. It was quiet except for an odd chirping sound similar to a large green frog with spots.

2. Elijah was excited for his first airplane ride. He was headed from Chicago, Illinois, to Los Angeles, California. The airport was extremely crowded with people. They were wearing winter coats of all colors: brown, black, pink, etc. He walked on the shiny floors. He smelled tacos, pizza, and hamburgers. He heard people talking, suitcases rolling on the ground, and announcements. Elijah, his mom, his dad, and his six-year-old sister, Nora, walked at a steady pace to Gate B12, which was on their left. Elijah sat down on a soft blue seat. They were thirty-two minutes early for their flight. His mom sat in the chair next to him as a woman across from him sneezed. "Are you nervous?" his mom asked. "A little," he said looking up at the bright lights all over the ceiling that were as white as a sheet of paper.

YOUR STORY

The following sentences have a different problem: they need *more* description. Rewrite the scenes, adding more details to make them stronger.

1. Jayden couldn't believe he was there. He finally was at a game! "Go Beavers!" he yelled.

2. Camy splashed Liam in the face. "I told you to stop!" he said. She left. He got out.

YOUR STORY

Mood (the feeling a story gives) and setting often go hand in hand. The words you choose to describe a setting can convey the mood of the scene. Write a detailed scenario for each of the following moods, characters, and settings. The first one is done for you.

MOOD: NERVOUS   **CHARACTER:** BOY   **SETTING:** PIANO RECITAL

The bright lights hurt Jamal's eyes. He looked out into the audience. It felt like every single person was staring at him, waiting for him to mess up. He put his fingers on the cold piano keys. It was so silent he could hear his heart beating out of his chest.

MOOD: LONELY   **CHARACTER:** FAIRY   **SETTING:** INSIDE A KITCHEN CABINET

MOOD:
CHEERFUL

CHARACTER:
GHOST

SETTING:
ABANDONED
MOVIE THEATER

_____

_____

_____

_____

MOOD:
GLOOMY

CHARACTER:
QUEEN BEE

SETTING:
BEEHIVE

_____

_____

_____

_____

YOUR STORY

Find a photo or picture from a magazine that has an interesting setting. Glue it right on this page and write a detailed description of it.

GLUE PICTURE HERE

YOUR STORY

Without revealing the picture, read the description you wrote in the preceding activity to a friend, and have them try to draw what they visualize. Did it end up looking like the picture? Are there details that would have helped make their drawing more accurate? Add those missing details to what you wrote. Maybe they came up with something even *cooler*—go ahead and add that to your Story Stash (page 28)!

"And nothing
teaches you
as much about
writing dialogue as
listening to it."

– JUDY BLUME

Here's a dare for you: spend the day in complete silence, not saying a word. How long do you think you'd last before you couldn't help but talk? I've lost my voice for over a week before. It was really tough not being able to communicate by talking to others!

Dialogue serves many purposes in stories. First, it helps move the story forward; we learn what is happening through the characters' conversations with one another. For instance, "Whoa! Did you just see that? What was it?" or "The volcano is starting to erupt! Run!"

Dialogue also gives us a taste of what the characters are like. Imagine the dialogue for a three-year-old vs. a neurobiology professor. Their interests (dolls vs. the cells of the nervous system), vocabulary, and sentence structure are completely different. Even their tones would vary. Imagine telling either of them to "Sit down a minute and relax" and how widely their reactions would differ. Realistic dialogue can make characters come to life.

You do want to be careful with giving too much *back-story* through dialogue, though. For example:

"Mateo, how *is* Oakwood Middle School—where we go to school?" I asked.

"Well, Allison Parker, I failed that test we took today. Mrs. Morris, our science teacher, was not happy with me."

Does that sound like a real conversation between two people who know each other well? Some information wouldn't need to be said, such as Mateo addressing Allison by her full name, or telling the name of their school or that Mrs. Morris was their science teacher. Both characters would already know these things. The author added these details for the reader's sake. Here is the same dialogue *without* the backstory:

"How was it?" I asked.

"I failed it—after all that work. Mrs. Morris was not happy."

You also want to avoid writing dialogue that isn't really needed:

"Hey," I said.

"How's it going?" Gianna asked.

"Well, okay I guess. What about you?"

Boring! I'm guilty of writing the beginning of scenes like this. My trick is to write it down (awful as it is) as it gets me to the good stuff. When I revise, I remove it. Often it really wasn't needed.

YOUR STORY

Pick three characters from a book or movie. Try to include one villain, such as Darth Vader. For each situation described below, write what you picture that character saying.

CHARACTER 1: _____

Situation: Trying to coax a cat from a tree

_____

_____

_____

_____

CHARACTER 2: _____

Situation: Teaching a caveman how to tie shoes

_____

_____

_____

_____

CHARACTER 3: _____

Situation: Telling a friend what they did over the weekend

_____

_____

_____

_____

YOUR STORY

Open up your favorite book and flip through it to find some of your favorite passages of dialogue. They can be funny, gross, sad, shocking—anything you like! Write them here. Flip back to this page when you need dialogue inspiration in the future.

_____

_____

_____

_____

_____

LISTENING CAREFULLY

"Go put your backpack away and wash your hands." Who do you think would say something like this: a mom or an eight-year-old boy? The words people use vary. What a parent says differs from what a child might say.

"I sighed. 'Do I have to? I. Just. Got. *Home*.'" Can we read into what this character is feeling from how they're saying it? Absolutely.

Two of your best tools for creating authentic dialogue are your ears. Listen to other people's conversations. I do this all the time, especially when I'm in the car. Because I can't see everyone talking, I only focus on what they're saying: the words they use, the pauses they take, the structure of their sentences.

If three of your best friends were standing behind you, could you tell who's talking based on word choices, pauses, and the structure of their sentences? Probably.

When I'm writing dialogue, I will actually read it aloud to see if it works. Does it sound like real people talking? If not, I need to keep working on it. A trick to see if your dialogue is working is to pick a random sentence a character is saying. Can you tell from just that quote who is saying it? If not, you may need to work on adding some little quirks into their dialogue.

YOUR STORY

Today you are going to be an undercover spy. Here is your secret assignment: write down a conversation you overhear. Of course, be sure it's nothing embarrassing or something you shouldn't be hearing. You could do this as your family is getting ready for bed or having breakfast on a Saturday. Write down what everyone says for a solid two minutes (it's longer than you think!). When you are done, reread it and note what makes each person's manner of speaking special to them. Do you notice any patterns?

YOUR STORY

The conversation you recorded in the previous activity might not have been super exciting. Can you think of any way to jazz it up? Let's try a word replacement game. Change a boring word to something more exciting. For instance, if your sister asked what you're having for dinner, change your dad's answer of "meatloaf" to "an ice-cream sundae bar." If your brother asked if the two of you could play outside, change "play outside" to "herd sheep." You can make a sentence silly with just a word or two tweaked. Use a different color pen to mark up your changes so they stand out.

JAZZ IT UP!

GETTING DIALOGUE JUST RIGHT

Can you add too much dialogue? Yes! I've been to plays where two characters are chatting for a whole scene without any background scenery or action taking place. I would have preferred some movement—something being stirred in a pot, a soft-shoe dance, even a character sweeping the floor! Be sure to break up what is being said with some action or setting detail to keep your readers engaged.

On the other hand, can there be too little dialogue? Absolutely. If your story sounds more like a summary of what's happening, add some dialogue. For instance, read the following:

Jack just finished setting up his lemonade stand when the first customer came by. It was a woman pulling kids in a wagon. The customer drank a glass of the lemonade. She got out her wallet. She liked the lemonade so much, she asked if she could buy the whole pitcher.

This sounds like an explanation of what happened (a summary) rather than the story itself. Let me add some dialogue:

"There. All set," Jack said, taping the last corner of his sign to the front of the table.

"Is that lemonade you're selling?" a woman asked, carting a wagon full of kids behind her.

"Yes. It's fifty cents. Would you like a glass?"

"Please."

Jack poured some into a cup.

The woman took a sip. "Wow! That's really good."

"I want some! I want some!" the kids whined.

The woman reached into her wallet. "You know what? We'll take all you have."

When you write, it's your job to try to balance every-thing: character detail, setting detail, plot, and dialogue.

YOUR STORY

Do you know how to format dialogue? Here's a quick quiz. The following sentences are about the rules of writing dialogue. Fill in the blanks using the words listed below.

COMMA   DIALOGUE   NEW   NOT   QUOTATION   PARAGRAPH

When writing dialogue:

1. Each time someone new is speaking, begin a new _____ .
2. Use _____ tags such as "she said" and "he asked" to help the reader know who's talking.
3. Use _____ marks around what someone is saying.
4. When using a dialogue tag, such as "he said" at the end of a sentence, add a _____ after the dialogue but before the end quotation marks: "I'm home," he said.
5. If the character's dialogue needs a second paragraph, you do _____ use end quotation marks at the end of the first paragraph. You will use quotation marks to start the _____ paragraph.

1. paragraph; 2. dialogue; 3. quotation; 4. comma; 5. not; new

YOUR STORY

Ready to write your own dialogue? Finish these scenes to make them more exciting.

SCENE 1

"Time to go to your sister's ballet recital," Mom said.

Jorge sighed. "Do I have to go?"

"Of course you do."

"Can't I just stay home?" Jorge asked.

"_____," Mom said.

SCENE 2

Willow looked across the yard, her fluffy tail twitching. The perfect acorn was smack in the middle of the Thompsons' yard. Willow scampered over to it. At the same time, a squirrel Willow had never met also darted to it.

_____

_____

_____

"I saw it first!" Jesse said, grabbing the baseball card from Wyatt.

"But it was my idea to even go to the card shop in the first place," Wyatt argued.

"So? You know I'm a bigger fan of Blake Johnson." Jesse was getting angrier by the second. He had been saving his allowance for that card for weeks.

"How can we figure out who gets it?"

YOUR STORY

See these characters? They're having a conversation. Think of a storyline for them, and then write the dialogue between them.

_____

_____

_____

_____

_____

_____

YOUR STORY

If you could invite three of your favorite celebrities to dinner, who would you invite? What would you talk about? What if you just learned the world is going to end in three hours and you all decide to spill any secrets you've kept? Time to have a conversation with them! What's nice about this fictional conversation is that the celebrities will say whatever you want them to. Don't forget to use the correct formatting for dialogue (see page 146) so we know who's saying what.

YOUR STORY

Anything you've been itching to write? Now's the time! You now know how to create a strong plot, rich characters, an exciting setting, and thrilling dialogue.

Take a good 20 minutes to focus on writing without turning on the TV or checking social media. If you're stuck on what to write about, look back at some of the other Your Story sections. If you run out of room, you can continue on your own paper.

PART 3

The End:
Happily Ever After

You have so many tools under your belt now to write a fabulous story. But you're not quite done. You have some big tasks ahead of you. First, be sure your story has an ending. It may make the reader say, "No! I can't believe you had that happen!" or "*Phew*. I'm so glad she's finally happy," or (hopefully) "I didn't see that coming!" You definitely don't want the reader to think "*That's* the end?" A satisfying ending makes the story a true winner.

Once your story is complete, are you done? No! Writing is an exciting adventure. You battled your way through the blank page, followed the trails of plot and character, established exciting settings, and ran through thrilling dialogue. And now you face the next step of the journey: the editing process!

YOUR STORY

Is there a book or movie you really liked but felt the ending fell flat? Write a new ending to it! Maybe instead of Cinderella marrying the prince, she decides to pack up her things and find her good friend Snow White, and they open up a bookstore together.

BOOK/MOVIE: _____

_____

_____

_____

_____

_____

_____

—

EDITING YOUR WORK

"When I finish the book, I take the first chapter and, without rereading it, throw it away. Then I write the first chapter last, now that I know how the story ends. It means I write the first chapter with confidence because the first chapter is the last chapter in disguise."

— RICHARD PECK

As a novelist, I know that when I finish *writing* my book, I am not nearly done. *Editing*, a careful reading and revising of what I wrote to make sure that everything makes sense and is correct, is a very important step. Editing often takes much longer than the actual writing of the story does. Even when I write a picture book, I spend many hours deciding what to change and how to change it.

I've *never* heard any author say that they wrote a book and didn't feel it needed any edits. There is always room for improvement. But how do you know what needs to be changed? It's not always easy.

Many authors share their work with others. I do this all the time. It's helpful because someone else reading it for the first time (with "fresh eyes," as they say) is better able to spot where my story isn't clear. Maybe I need to describe the setting in more detail. Or maybe the ending wasn't satisfying. It might be hard for me to figure that out on my own. I also appreciate when someone else identifies words or sentences that can be cut. It only makes my story stronger.

It's also important to edit your own work (this is called *self-editing*). Here are some things to look for:

- **Does your story have a clear beginning, middle, and end?**
- **Is your main character well developed? Do we get a sense of who they are?**
- **Have you described the setting in enough detail?**
- **Do you have the right amount of dialogue?**
- **Have you used the strongest word choices you can (instead of "ran quickly" perhaps use "sprinted")?**
- **Have you taken out any unnecessary words or sentences?**
- **Have you checked for spelling errors?**
- **Have you checked for grammatical errors?**

Errors can distract a reader from your story, and you don't want that.

YOUR STORY

Can you think of other things you want to include in the self-edit list? Add them here.

-
-
-
-

YOUR STORY

Writers often unknowingly repeat the same (and often unneeded) words in their writing. My go-to words are "so" (*Eeek!* I just did a search: I have over 100 in the novel I'm writing!), "other," "more," and "again." Other overused words include "got," "many," and "well." The passive verbs "is/are/was/were/am" (I am, he is, etc.) also make their way into my stories more often than they should. Always attempt to reword the sentence with a stronger, more active verb when you can.

Take a look at a story you've written. Do an inventory by circling and counting up how many times you use the following words:

again: _____ **times**

got: _____ **times**

is/are/was/were/am: _____ **times**

many: _____ **times**

more: _____ **times**

other: _____ **times**

so: _____ **times**

well: _____ **times**

YOUR STORY

How did you do in the preceding exercise? Are you surprised at how many times you used a particular word? Choose one of your overused words. See if you can edit your sentences, getting rid of that word. It's probably not as easy as just removing the word; you will likely need to rework the sentence. But that's all part of writing, isn't it? Use a different colored pen to edit your story.

YOUR STORY

Did you know there are people called "editors" whose job is to edit authors' work? Practice your editing skills on the following passage. Add detail where needed. See if there are any unnecessary words you can cross out. Last, check for grammar and spelling errors.

"Wow, look at that fish! Axel said to Sam, pointing to the fish in the really hudge fish tank. There were three other people looking at it. They were smileing and talking about the big baseball game the night before.

And that one!"

"I"ll bet there's six different kinds of fish in there."

"Hey, where'd our group go?" Sam asked.

Axel and sam looked for the rest of their field trip group but they didn't see anyone.

"Since I was trying so hard to make books lead my life, I didn't want to read them and then just put them back on the shelf and say, 'good book,' as if I was patting a good dog. I wanted books to change me, and I wanted to write books that would change others."

– FROM *HOLE IN MY LIFE* BY JACK GANTOS

THE PLOT THICKENS

I write seven days a week. I don't do that because I have to. I do it because I enjoy it. There are times when you're required to write something—maybe an essay for school or a thank-you note for a gift. But when you write personal pieces, it should be about having fun. If it feels like a chore, stop. Take a break. Do something else: feed the fish, practice your disco moves—anything. If you feel like writing later, do so. Otherwise, revisit it another time.

You may even begin a story and find that it's just not working for you. That's okay! Put it aside. Authors call this "putting the story in a drawer." You literally hide it away for a while and then revisit it when you feel refreshed. I don't advise throwing away any story for good. Ever! You never know when you'll have an *aha* moment and want to look at it again. I've actually put a story to the side for years before working on it again.

YOUR STORY

This is a two-part prompt. Today, just do this part. Tomorrow, complete the prompt that immediately follows this one.

Write a few paragraphs on the following topic: Your character is in a candy store and accidentally bumps over a display of candy. The candy spills all over the floor.

_____

_____

_____

_____

_____

_____

_____

_____

_____

_____

_____

_____

_____

_____

_____

_____

_____

YOUR STORY

Is it tomorrow yet? No cheating! Read what you wrote yesterday. Now that you've given yourself some time away from it, can you spot anything you can improve? Go back through it with a colored pen (use a different color) and find ways to make your writing stronger.

YOUR STORY

Want to rev up a story? Pick one you wrote earlier and change each character to an animal! The characters can either be one type of animal—maybe a quiver of cobras, a memory of elephants, or a bloat of hippos—or each person can be a different animal (the mom: a lemur; the dad: a jellyfish; a friend: a swan; you: ?). What do you need to change about the story or dialogue? Sometimes editing can have a ripple effect, so consider the effects of any changes on your whole story.

YOUR STORY

Each sentence counts, so be sure yours are the strongest they can be. Sometimes playing with how you say something can drastically improve your story. You can:

- **add more detail to a sentence**
- **break up the sentence into multiple, shorter sentences**
- **change up the order**
- **add dialogue**
- **replace a verb with a stronger one**

The possibilities are endless! For instance, take the sentence

"The mouse was grabbed by the giant and gobbled up."

How can I change it?

1. The giant grabbed the mouse and gobbled it up.
2. The giant reached into the mouse hole, pulled out the little rodent, and gobbled him up.
3. "Got you now!" the giant said, grabbing the mouse and shoving him into his mouth.
4. The mouse couldn't resist the giant's strong grip and ended up being a light dinner.

I could go on forever, but I'll let you try instead.

Take the following sentence and write down six different ways to say the same thing:

"The girl climbed up the tree and looked down."

1. _____

_____

2. _____

_____

3. _____

_____

4. _____

_____

5. _____

_____

6. _____

_____

GO, GO, GO!

"If you don't see
the book you want
on the shelves, write it."

– BEVERLY CLEARY

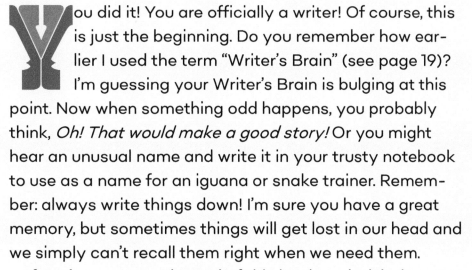

You did it! You are officially a writer! Of course, this is just the beginning. Do you remember how earlier I used the term "Writer's Brain" (see page 19)? I'm guessing your Writer's Brain is bulging at this point. Now when something odd happens, you probably think, *Oh! That would make a good story!* Or you might hear an unusual name and write it in your trusty notebook to use as a name for an iguana or snake trainer. Remember: always write things down! I'm sure you have a great memory, but sometimes things will get lost in our head and we simply can't recall them right when we need them.

If you've come to the end of this book and wish there was more, don't fret! Many of the prompts can be done over and over again on different paper. If you don't already own a notebook for your writing, put it on your next birthday wish list. Whatever you do, keep on writing! The more you write, the stronger you get.

YOUR STORY

Now that you are officially a writer with a big Writer's Brain, record the titles to three stories you plan to write. Draw the cover of each book in the spaces provided.

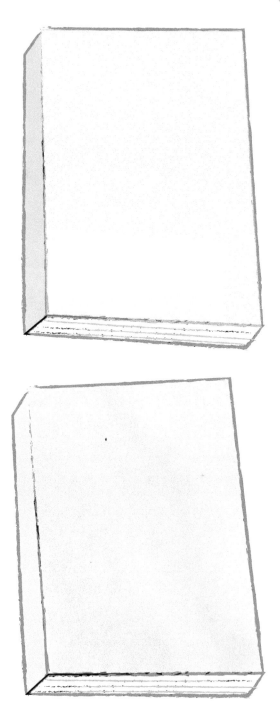

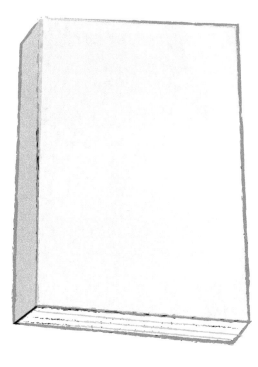

YOUR STORY

Need more inspiration? Here is a wide array of subjects you could write about. Circle the ones that interest you.

BROOM HOCKEY   tightrope walker

A SHRINKING MACHINE

glowworms   black

sandcastles   holes

SECRET CODES

a world without
technology   invisibility

Smell-O-Vision   gnomes   WORLD

(it was a real thing!)   creepy things   PEACE

volcanoes

YOUR STORY

Time to narrow down the choices you made in the previous activity! Choose two topics you circled and merge them together to create a brand-new story.

YOUR STORY

You know those movies where two characters switch lives? If you could switch lives with anyone, who would it be? Your sibling? A trillionaire? A ninja? Choose one person to switch lives with and write one scene about it.

YOUR STORY

Interview time! Say hello to . . . *yourself!* Now that you've spent a lot of time thinking about writing, fill out the following questionnaire about what you've learned about yourself.

1. My writing strengths are creating characters/describing settings/writing exciting plots/inventing dialogue. *(circle all that apply)*

2. I need to work more on creating tension/adding the right balance of dialogue/editing. *(circle only one)*

3. I can work on this by reading other novels and noticing how other authors do it/writing more/_____.
   (circle all that apply)

4. A topic I never thought I'd write on but am now interested in is _____.

5. I am more interested in writing short stories/novels/graphic novels/fantasy/historical fiction than I used to be. *(circle all that apply)*

6. Something I learned about myself after reading this book is:

_____

_____

_____

INDEX

ACKNOWLEDGMENTS

Books often include a page where the author thanks those people who have helped in creating the book—and this is mine!

First, I would like to thank my children for being my muses—their lives help me think of many story ideas, including ones in this book. I also have to thank all of my teachers from my hometown of Waukegan, Illinois, who always encouraged me to write. I'm still in touch with some of them. Mrs. Clark and Mrs. Adee, you helped me develop writing tools (and my love of writing) that I was able to share in this book.

I would also like to thank my editor, Alyson Penn at Callisto. She helped me tighten up my wording, made my ideas stronger, and gave great suggestions throughout.

YOUR STORY

Who would you like to thank for being the writer you are? Write your "Acknowledgments" page here.

_____

_____

_____

_____

_____

ABOUT THE AUTHOR

NATALIE ROMPELLA is the author of over 60 books and materials for kids, including the middle grade novel *Cookie Cutters & Sled Runners*, and two insect books—the newest being *The World Never Sleeps*. She lives in the Chicago suburbs with her husband, two kids, and dog. When she's not writing, she enjoys playing pickleball, doing Zumba, and collecting insects. Weird, huh?

YOUR STORY

Write your "About the Author" page. Include the number of stories you've written, where you live, who's in your family, and other interests. You can even add a photo of yourself below!

CPSIA information can be obtained
at www.ICGtesting.com
Printed in the USA
BVHW051631130721
611263BV00003B/4